THE BACKY

ANSWER GUIDE

By Bill Thompson, III, and the editors of *Bird Watcher's Digest*

CONTENTS

Front cover: *Eastern screech-owl from W. Greene/VIREO.*

Above: *White-winged dove* by Ned Harris.

THE BACKYARD BIRD WATCHER'S ANSWER GUIDE was produced by the staff of *Bird Watcher's Digest*: Bill Thompson, III, *Booklet Editor and Booklet Concept*; Andy Thompson, *Publisher, BWD Press;* Durrae Johanek, *Editorial Consultant;* Deborah Griffith, *Assistant Editor;* Andy Stout, and Claire Mullen, *Production Director.*

Bird Watcher's Digest is published by Pardson Corporation, P.O. Box 110, Marietta, OH 45750. To order additional copies of *THE BACKYARD BIRD WATCHER'S ANSWER GUIDE,* or our other booklets, or for *BWD* subscription information, call us toll-free 800-879-2473 or visit **birdwatchersdigest.com** on the Internet.
ISBN # 1-880241-16-1.

General Bird Questions

Lifespan

Q: How long do birds live? P.L., OHIO

A: *An Introduction to Ornithology* by George Wallace and Harold D. Mahan states that the mean natural longevity of wild birds is very low. The potential of longer life can be realized by considering the life spans of captive birds in species well adjusted to captivity such as parrots, pigeons, and swans. (Note: No wild bird may be held captive without the proper federal permits.) There are many records of banded wild passerines living 10 to 20 years and nonpasserines for more than 10, but computed averages usually are for fewer than 2 years.

Sleep

Q: Where do birds go at night? K.B., NEW HAMPSHIRE

A: Most birds roost (sleep) in the same sorts of habitat in which they spend their days. Cavity-nesting birds tend to sleep in roosting holes (or nest boxes); downy, hairy, and red-cockaded woodpeckers build roosting holes in the fall (which eventually become nesting cavities for other birds and animals). Some water birds roost in their element; however, many herons roost in trees, as do pheasants; other species roost in shrubbery, out of reach of predators.

Christopher Leahy, in *The Birdwatcher's Companion,* notes that birds that are gregarious during their nesting season (herons, ibises, gulls and terns, swifts) often sleep in large groups. Some roosts may contain a single species, but they are frequently mixed.

Horned larks, partridges, and quail roost on the ground; ruffed grouse are known to roost in snowbanks for warmth in winter.

Q: When birds sleep on a wire, why don't they tip over? J.S., KENTUCKY

A: Birds' feet have tendons that hold them closed, locked in a clinging or gripping position, when the leg is flexed, as it is when a bird crouches. This allows birds to perch and rest without falling or losing their grip.

Death and populations

Q: What happens to dead birds? K.M., GEORGIA

A: Injured or sick birds seek cover in which to die, and are rarely found. Raccoons, opossums, and skunks form a cleanup crew. Ants will strip a carcass clean in 24 to 48 hours, leaving no more than a small skull in evidence of the original kill. Larger carcasses take ants and other scavengers more time to clean up.

Q: I don't see as many birds as I used to. What's happening? C.T., COLORADO

A: Three factors may be at work. First, bird populations naturally fluctuate over time. Second, local

TOM VEZO

Large flocks of blackbirds form in the fall. These flocks feed in agricultural fields and often descend on backyard feeding stations.

bird populations change with changing land uses. A meadow converted to houses, driveways, and lawns will not support meadowlarks. And third, human activity is homogenizing our bird life. Blue jays, robins, and grackles (all birds that thrive in suburban yards) are doing fine. Thrushes, vireos, and warblers, which require woodland habitat, are struggling.

Identification help

Q: A strange-looking bird has been coming to my feeder. How can I identify it? H.L., IOWA

A: A good place to start is to note the two or three most obvious things you notice about the strange bird. Start at the top of the head and move downward and back toward the tail, noting the bird's "field marks." Next, check this list against images in a field guide. Check your local library, bookstore, or the Internet for a field guide to the birds of your area. *Bird Watcher's Digest's* booklet, *An Identification Guide to Common Backyard Birds*, might also be helpful. (See this booklet's outside back cover.)

Deformed bills

Q: What causes deformed bills on birds? A mourning dove with an odd-looking bill comes to my feeder. L.E., MICHIGAN

A: Deformities can be caused by several factors including injury, natural genetic mutation, genetic inbreeding, and exposure to certain chemicals during embryonic development. In short, even if all the dioxin, PCBs, and DDT-like pesticides disappeared, birds would still occasionally appear with deformed bills.

Bad weather

Q: I had plans to go birding recently, but high winds kept me home. What do birds do when it's windy? M.B., MARYLAND

A: Birds have many coping behaviors. They face the wind so moving air does not ruffle their feathers, thereby robbing them of the insulating heat layer between feathers and skin. Facing the wind also presents their naturally aerodynamic shape, which gives the least resistance. They stay on or low to the ground where actual wind speed is lower, and in the lee of any objects that can deflect the wind: tree trunks, power poles, fenceposts, shrubs, grass clumps, buildings. Birds also move as little as possible, thus conserving energy. Because they keep to dense cover, birding in high winds may be a bird-free proposition.

Finding food and feeders

Q: How do birds find new feeding stations? One bird appears, then more individuals of the same species, and soon other species appear. How does the word get spread? B.B., COLORADO

A: Birds are highly mobile creatures, adapted to finding and taking advantage of changing food supplies. Studies have shown that vocal and visual clues are used to locate food. For example, a bird flying over an area of great activity, such as a feeding station, will be attracted by the noise and movements of those birds feeding below. Flocking species, such as finches and blackbirds, may be alerted to a food source by one individual. In winter, many small woodland species such as chickadees, nuthatches, kinglets, woodpeckers, and creepers form loose-knit feeding flocks that range about, benefiting from the extra eyes a flock provides in locating food and spotting predators.

Attracting bluebirds

Q: How can I attract more bluebirds to my yard? M.S., MISSOURI

A: Like most songbirds, nesting bluebirds defend territories against other birds of their own kind. You can only pack so many sardines into a can, and you can pack only so many bluebirds into an acre of habitat. The best recourse is to evangelize your neighbors and get them to develop or preserve bluebird habitat, too. Bluebirds prefer large open expanses of grass or meadow with convenient hunting perches scattered throughout.

Plumage differences

Q: I was watching three female cardinals on our bird feeder. Two had red bills, the other a dark or black bill. Why the difference? A.L., MICHIGAN

A: Bird identification also involves recognizing species, sex, age, seasonal changes, geographic nuances, genetic variation, and sometimes physical interaction with the bird's environment.

Some common examples are

A leucistic (partial albino) female northern cardinal.

RON ALSTING

tanagers that are red in summer but green in winter, yellow-shafted flickers in the East and red-shafted flickers in the West, red and gray morphs of the eastern screech-owl, and iron compounds in water that stain the necks of swans and snow geese. Without knowing these circumstances, a person could easily look at two individuals of the same species and presume them to be different species. What you saw were the effects of sex and age. The birds with red bills were adult female cardinals, and the bird with the dark bill was an juvenile cardinal.

Q: A flock of about 12 house finches feeds daily at my window bird feeder. Most are the usual red house finches, but I also have a couple that are definitely orange and at least one that is very yellow. Why the color differences? D.M., CALIFORNIA

A: Research published in 1931 clearly linked age with color in house finches. Scientists were able to determine that younger male house finches tend to be lighter colored (yellow and orange). In 1976, experimental results that linked color with diet were published. Presuming older males are more experienced at finding, recognizing, and competing for food, younger and older males, even though they feed together, may not have identical diets. This explains why mixed colors would appear in the same flock.

"Albino" birds

Q: I saw an unusual robin with a white head. It seemed to be healthy and was with a flock of robins who were pecking around in the newly mown grass in a pecan grove. There's no doubt at all that it was one of the robins: fat tummy, red breast, and all. Was it partially albino? K.S., OHIO

Q: What is the name for the condition that our "variegated grackle" has? He appeared at one of our feeders briefly a few weeks ago. Is this partial albinism? M.G., IOWA

A: Both of these birds could be described as partial albinos, but the correct term is leucistic. Partial albinism, or leucism, can be caused by poor diet, physical trauma to the affected area, or a genetic defect. The term albino is reserved for totally white creatures with pink flesh/soft part colors (bills, facial skin, and legs) and eyes.

Discarded eggshells

Q: What happens to eggshells after birds hatch? C.P., KANSAS

A: Some birds leave their nests soon after hatching, so their eggshells usually just get left behind. For those birds that remain in the nest for a while, the parent birds either remove the eggshells, carrying them some distance from the nest, or eat them.

In either case, many mammals and a few birds ultimately eat the eggshells, from which they get such essential nutrients as phosphorus, magnesium, potassium, and calcium.

Martins and green leaves

Q: I recently saw purple martins picking leaves from a persimmon tree and apparently taking them to their nests. For what purpose do martins use green leaves? R.M., CONNECTICUT

A: Martins may line nests with green leaves because aromatic compounds in the leaves facilitate nest cleaning and help reduce nest-dwelling parasites.

How birds drink

Q: While watching birds at the water in my feeding area, I saw that most birds dip their bills, then immediately tilt their heads up. Mourning doves hold their bills in the water for a brief period during which the throat pulses as if swallowing. How do birds drink? Do mourning doves and other birds differ? H.B., WISCONSIN

A: You've made a good observation. Mourning doves do drink differently from other birds. In fact, swallowing water with the head down and bill immersed is an ability shared only by the approximately 300 species in the dove family and the northern fulmar. All other birds that drink (not all do) take water into the mouth then tilt the head up so the water trickles down the throat.

Unusual diets

Q: For the past few weeks I have had a seed-eating robin at my feeder. All robins I have ever seen eat bugs, worms, and/or berries. Is this seed-eater unusual? J.H., ARKANSAS

A: Robins are so adaptable that they can survive almost anywhere. Part of their adaptability is a willingness to eat diverse foods. Robins are masters at finding and eating whatever food is available. Their diet may be as varied as that of American crows.

Hawks at feeders

Q: We observed a sharp-shinned hawk eating a bird in our yard. After the hawk left, I checked the remains and found the victim was a house sparrow. We didn't see the hawk catch the bird, but this is the third sighting I've had of the hawk in our yard in two weeks. How commonly do sharp-shinned hawks hunt in backyard areas? L.G., A.L., MISSOURI

A: Sharp-shinned hawks find mature urban woodlands more suitable for their lifestyle. In some areas, they can be more easily found in urban-suburban complexes than in surrounding rural areas, suggesting adaptation to human-created landscapes and feeding stations.

Bird Feeding

When to feed

Q: What is the best time of year to put out a feeder? C.M., ALABAMA

A: The best time to place a feeder is anytime. In spring you'd be smart to put out a hummingbird feeder with a sugar-water mix of four parts water to one part sugar.

Fall and winter are the best times for seed feeders. Use tube feeders filled with black-oil sunflower seed or sunflower hearts. It may take a few weeks or longer for birds to find the feeders, but they will find them. For expert advice on bird feeding, see our backyard booklet series. (Refer to outside back cover.)

ROBERT McCAW

A male house finch joins four male American goldfinches at a tube feeder filled with black-oil sunflower seed.

The best seed

Q: What is the best seed to offer birds? P.G., VIRGINIA

A: Black-oil sunflower seed is the most universally eaten seed at bird feeders, but there are many other seeds and foods to offer. What is most popular with your birds depends on where you live and what birds are present. For more bird-feeding tips, check out our backyard booklet *Enjoying Bird Feeding More.* (See the outside back cover.)

Best feeder

Q: What is the best bird feeder? F.S., Maryland

A: There is no single best bird feeder. A well-rounded feeding operation will include a platform feeder, a tube feeder, a hopper feeder, a suet feeder, and a peanut feeder. And don't forget the birdbath! For the best advice on feeders and food for birds, consult one of these publications: *Enjoying Bird Feeding More*, by Julie Zickefoose, *Bird Watching For Dummies*, by Bill Thompson, III, or *A Guide to Western Bird Feeding*, by John V. Dennis. Ask for these at your local retail store or visit **www.birdwatchersdigest.com**.

Cats and birds

Q: What can I do to protect the birds in my yard from cats?

D.B., MAINE

A: Hang feeders at least five feet above the ground. For ground-feeding birds, arrange ornamental border fencing in two or three concentric circles about 16 inches to two feet apart, to disrupt a cat's ability to leap at feeders or to spring on birds. Harass offending cats with a spray of water to train them to avoid your yard. If all else fails, use a live trap to catch the cats and take them to the local animal shelter. If the cats belong to your neighbors, ask them to restrain their pets from accessing your yard.

Cleaning feeders

Q: How often must I clean my bird feeders and what should I use? K.D., COLORADO

A: Every two to fours weeks, clean and disinfect your feeders. Use hot, soapy water and a rag on plastic models and a soft-bristled brush on wooden feeders. After removing all debris, rinse the feeder with clear water. Mix one capful of liquid chlorine bleach for each gallon of tepid warm water in a bucket or tub large enough to immerse the feeder for one minute. Let it dry and refill it. Note: Adding more bleach won't necessarily increase disinfection but may damage feeders.

Stopping starlings

Q: What kind of feeder will discourage starlings? E.B., Alabama

A: Tube feeders seem to work best at making life difficult for starlings. This species is incredibly adaptable. You may want to stop feeding peanuts, mixed seed, bread products, table scraps, and suet for a few days to discourage starlings. Try limiting your feeding to black-oil sunflower seed.

Pigeon problems

Q: How do I get rid of pigeons without harming blue jays, cardinals, grackles, woodpeckers, and squirrels? E.R., FLORIDA

A: • Watch what they eat and quit serving it until they stop visiting.

• Don't put feed on the ground or use ledges, platforms, or any flat surfaces. Use only hanging feeders that sway and feeders too small for the rock pigeons.

• Keep all excess food cleaned up off the ground.

• Lure the rock pigeons away from your main feeding area by putting their preferred food someplace where you can tolerate them.

• Discourage these pigeons from roosting nearby by using chickenwire to screen off roosting sites.

Foiling sparrows

Q: House sparrows have learned how to get into my suet block. They hang from the bottom of the wire-caged, top-covered, hanging block just like chickadees. Any suggestions for keeping this food source available to the less aggressive species? B.S., WASHINGTON

A: Three combined actions might help:

First, insert a spring in the line from which you hang the suet block. It should be tighter than a slinky but flexible enough to allow some bobbing action triggered by the weight of a small bird. Swinging and twisting motions combined with up-and-down motion usually

ROB & ANN SIMPSON

Common grackles can dominate feeders at times. To discourage them, discontinue offering mixed seed.

discourage everything except downy woodpeckers, chickadees, siskins, and goldfinches.

Second, hang more than one suet block. Decoy house sparrows away from your main feeding area with a stationary suet block close to the ground.

Third, reduce the number of house sparrows in your neighborhood by eliminating access to protected nesting sites. Watch the sparrows in spring, and they'll show you where those sites are. In extreme cases, sparrow traps such as those sold by the Purple Martin Conservation Association (814-734-4420 or **www.purplemartin.org**) can be used to live-trap house sparrows.

Foiling blackbirds

Q: Red-winged blackbirds and grackles have taken over my feeders. My feeders are kind of large. Should I change to smaller feeders or is there a better method? C.T., OKLAHOMA

A: Your best bet is to switch to tube feeders and to eliminate feeding on the ground. Feed only black-oil sunflower seed for the time being: no mixed seed or cracked corn. Blackbirds at feeders are largely a fall and winter phenomenon. Once spring migration starts, the large blackbird flocks start to break up and head north.

Q: I read that starlings, blackbirds, and grackles do not like safflower seeds but smaller birds (titmice, chickadees) do. Is this true? And if so, will it keep the larger birds from cleaning out our feeders before the smaller ones can get to it? A.A., COLORADO

A: Some blackbirds will only eat safflower when there's nothing else to eat. Cardinals seem to love it. If you want to feed smaller birds, get small, roofed feeders that exclude the larger birds (satellite-shaped feeders and domed feeders work well). These feeders have adjustable roofs that prevent larger birds from accessing the food.

Hawks at feeders

Q: How can I discourage the hawk that has been stalking my feeders? B.C., NORTH DAKOTA

A: Accipiters (Cooper's and sharp-shinned hawks are two) are bird-eating hawks that commonly visit feeding stations. You can't prevent these predators from hunting in your yard, but here are some things you can do to encourage them to look for easier meals elsewhere.

- Create shelter and escape habitat for the feeder birds, using shrubs, trees, brush piles, and brushy areas.
- Move your feeders from the middle of an open area and place them nearer to cover so it's harder for a hawk to surprise and catch birds.
- Quit feeding for a time to encourage all birds to disperse.

Impact of feeding

Q: Is bird feeding bad for birds? O.A., TENNESSEE

A: Yes and no. Certainly some bird species (house finches, cardinals, house sparrows, starlings) have prospered from the food at feeders, but feeding has not had a dramatic positive effect on overall bird populations.

However, because they concentrate lots of birds, feeders have been the source of several outbreaks of avian disease. When sick birds intermingle with healthy birds, the disease spreads. In addition, feeding has helped certain nonnative species (house sparrows, European starlings, rock pigeons, house finches in the East) thrive at the expense of native species. To avoid transmitting disease, practice good feeder hygiene: Clean your feeders once a month with a bleach-water solution (one cup bleach to two gallons water). Feed only as much food as your birds will eat in a day. If you see sick or dead birds at your feeder, notify your local wildlife officials and stop feeding for a few weeks. This forces the birds to disperse and lessens the chances that any disease will spread among them.

Q: If I stop feeding the birds in my backyard, will they starve? M.G., NEW JERSEY

A: No. Birds are not totally reliant on the food offered at feeding stations. Birds have evolved over millions of years to be very mobile in their food-finding habits. Feeding stations have been linked to slightly improved survival rates for birds in very harsh weather conditions, but, overall, bird feeding does not drastically affect the birds' survival.

Stopping squirrels

Q: I've read that putting hot peppers in birdseed prevents squirrels from eating the seed. Doesn't this harm the birds? K.J., OHIO

A: Although some birds naturally eat chili peppers in the wild, they swallow them whole, and they are neutralized by stomach acid. Ground chili peppers can burn the throat and esophagus on the way down, and at the very least, there is the danger to the birds of inhalation and eye contact.

Q: How do I keep squirrels off my bird feeders? P.T., CONNECTICUT

A: Baffling your feeders (preventing squirrels from gaining access to the feeders) is the best way. Hang them from a thin wire, far from any object from

A red squirrel at a feeder.

ROBERT McCAW

which the squirrels can leap. String the wire with empty 35mm film canisters (lids on), that will spin and dump the squirrels off. There are many squirrel-proof feeders on the market that may give the squirrels a small electric shock, prevent them from reaching the seed, or rotate or bounce to dump the squirrels off. But be forewarned: Squirrels have been known to outsmart the most ingenious of squirrel proof inventions.

If you can't beat 'em, join 'em. Feed squirrels ears of dried corn, but place the corn away from your bird feeders. Given the choice, squirrels will always go for the easiest food, and they *love* corn. For more information on feeding or defeating backyard squirrels, check out the BWD Press booklet *Enjoying Squirrels More (or Less)*. (See this booklet's outside back cover.)

Offering eggshells

Q: Is it necessary to bake eggshells for birds, and why do they like or need them? T.A., CALIFORNIA

A: The eggshells are baked in an oven for a half hour at 350 degrees to kill off any bacteria left from the egg residue. The heat kills any nasty stuff that might make the birds sick. Birds eat the eggshells for the calcium they provide. During the egg-laying season female birds need to replace calcium lost in egg production. Eggshells are a great source of this important mineral.

Thistle feeders and finches

Q: Early in spring I put out two thistle feeders in my yard. At first I had a lot of finches, but they disappeared and just returned about a week ago. My friend in Ohio has finches year-round. Do these finches migrate north in hot weather? M.G., TENNESSEE

A: During times of abundant natural food such as seeds, berries, nuts, fruits, and insects, many feeder birds roam widely, taking advantage of the bounty. A few birds will visit your feeders during these times, but many more will join them as the natural food supplies dwindle in fall. In winter, when natural food supplies are at their lowest, more birds take advantage of food at feeding stations.

Spillage

Q: What can I do to keep the wind from blowing all the food out of my hanging feeders? I have tube feeders that swing so much in the wind that the food spills out in no time. S.B., SOUTH CAROLINA

A: Various strategies can minimize the problem. Because wind direction is somewhat seasonally predictable, having alternative sites for hanging your bird feeders can help. Try the following tips singly or in combination.

• Hang feeders in the lee of a shrub thicket. The birds like to have cover nearby as shelter from predators and wind, and will use the thicket for roosting.

• Attach your feeders to the lee side of your house, a fence, or close to a tree trunk.

• Switch to pole-mounted feeders during windy weather. The wind will still blow some food to the ground, but sparrows, cardinals, juncos, doves, towhees, and a few other birds prefer feeding on the ground anyway.

• Take down your feeders until the wind subsides. Birds are not as active in high winds and they will return when the wind dies down.

Moths in seed

Q: In an opened bag of black-oil sunflower seed I was dismayed to find a great profusion of little moths, some dead, some not, lots of little larvae, webby material, etc., in with the seed. How can we prevent this? Is there anything we could apply to the seed after purchase to get rid of bugs and yet do no harm to birds? M.B., INDIANA

A: Try not to buy more food than you'll use in a season. If you do overestimate, don't worry about the surplus and don't bother treating it. Those spiders we grind under foot or flush down the toilet, wrens savor as gourmet food. And, you probably know, robins eat worms. The birds will eat the bugs as readily as the seed. Your seed was likely infested with Indian meal moths. Next feeding season, stick a few handfuls of bay leaves in your seed container. Bay leaves have a natural insect-repelling property.

Feeding bluebirds

Q: Eastern bluebirds do not eat any of the seed or suet that I offer during winter. What can I feed them? J.G., GEORGIA

A: Some insectivorous birds will eat feeder fare and some won't. Bluebirds generally stick to insects. They would rather move around to find insects than to change their diet to other available food. When snow cover makes insects difficult to find, they might eat mealworms, peanut butter, suet, or sunflower hearts.

According to *Enjoying Bluebirds More*, published by BWD Press, your best chance to attract winter bluebirds is to provide fruiting trees (such as dogwood, American holly, cedar, sassafras, juniper, and shadbush) and shrubs (such as bayberry, red-osier dogwood, deciduous holly, pokeweed, and sumac) on which bluebirds rely in winter. Providing water year-round is another great attractant for bluebirds and other species.

Bald cardinals

Q: I have two bald cardinals at my feeders. Why are they bald? Is it something I'm feeding? B.H., NORTH CAROLINA

A: Your cardinals are either young birds with head feathers still developing, or they are victims of avian feather mites that eat the feathers and cause the birds to "go bald." The mites exist on the birds in the only place the birds cannot preen themselves—on the head. In one month or so you should have no bald cardinals because the birds will have molted in a new set of

HUGH P. SMITH JR.

Bluebirds will come to feeding stations for suet, raisins, grapes, peanut bits, and mealworms. This is a male western bluebird.

feathers. The mites are perfectly natural, not caused by diet, and relatively harmless, unless the bird is in an otherwise-weakened state.

Seed hulls killing grass

Q: Our backyard feeder is easily emptied by the birds. This causes a carpet of uneaten birdseed on our lawn that kills the grass. We have tried other feeders, but either the birds can empty them just as easily or won't use them at all. Most of the birds are sparrows and finches, with the sparrows being the ones that spill the seed out of the feeder. Is there a type of feeder or attachable catch tray to prevent wasted seed? S.B., SOUTH DAKOTA

A: If you are getting lots of seed buildup, not just hulls but actual seed, you are probably overfeeding. Cut back. Put out a little bit of food every day instead of a lot of food once every few days.

If you are feeding wild bird mix, the birds might be raking at the millet and cracked corn to find sunflower seeds. Try feeding straight black-oil sunflower seed and just a little mixed seed.

Clean the ground beneath your feeders on a weekly basis. Otherwise, you will encourage *Aspergillus* fungi and *Salmonella* bacteria, both of which can kill birds.

Once you've addressed these points, check the specialty bird stores and catalogs for snap-on seed-catching trays for tube feeders.

Finches and sunflowers

Q: American goldfinches feeding in my yard seem to prefer picking their own food from my live sunflower plants as opposed to loose seed in the feeders. In addition to commercial sunflower seed, I also always keep plenty of thistle (Niger) seed available. What can I do? J.H., NEW JERSEY

A: Long before the first bird feeders were hung and the first seeds were bagged for sale, goldfinches and sunflowers were forging bonds. You have witnessed the natural consequences of hundreds of thousands of generations of contact between plant and bird. Later in the year, when the natural seed crop is depleted, the goldfinches will be more likely to visit your feeders.

Nest Boxes/Nesting

Nesting time

Q: I recently put up a bluebird box in my backyard. In early November I noticed several bluebirds inspecting this box. Do bluebirds lay eggs at this time of year? Will they use this for a winter home? M.A., LOUISIANA

A: Like other songbirds in North America, bluebirds nest during spring and summer. Your bluebirds were looking for roosting space for the winter and potential nesting space for next spring.

Why no birds?

Q: My son and husband made a birdhouse for me and set it on a pole. It's been up for a while, but no birds are going in it. Is this normal or did they do something wrong? L.W., RHODE ISLAND

A: First, make sure the entry hole is at least 1½ inches across. This is the optimum size to admit wrens, chickadees, titmice, bluebirds, and tree swallows.

Only those birds that use tree cavities will use birdhouses. Of approximately 850 bird species in North America, less than an eighth of them nest or roost in tree cavities. Some of these birds are much too large to use a birdhouse.

Also, some cavity-nesting birds leave your area in the winter. They simply aren't there to use your birdhouse until spring.

Many cavity-nesting birds, such as woodpeckers, insist on making their own cavities and won't use a birdhouse.

A few birds will roost in birdhouses during harsh weather, but will not use the same birdhouse for nesting or roosting during nice weather.

Some birds that might use a birdhouse don't nest in urban or suburban areas. If you live in a rural area, those same birds are more likely to use your birdhouse.

For more information, read *A Guide to Bird Homes* by Scott Shalaway. (See this booklet's outside back cover.)

RON AUSTING

House wrens and bluebirds

Q: Is it true that wrens can eject young bluebirds from their houses? I would like to place both a wren house and a bluebird house on my property, but I do not want to create a conflict. I currently have wrens visit my feeders, but no bluebirds. B.R., INDIANA

A: The wrens you are seeing at your suet are probably Carolina wrens, which can co-exist with bluebirds. The wrens that cause problems are house wrens, which migrate south for the winter and return in April and May to set up territories. Place your bluebird houses in the middle of a large grassy area, such as a meadow or large lawn. Locate your wren houses along the edge of the trees or woods. This will keep the house

Five hungry nestlings gape to be fed as this male eastern bluebird enters the nest box with food.

wrens and bluebirds from fighting over housing.

Carolina wrens

Q: Carolina wrens have left one egg on consecutive mornings in the decoration hanging on our front door, but we never see any wrens sitting on the eggs. Is this normal? L.T., PENNSYLVANIA

A: Yes, it is normal when the female is completing a clutch of eggs. Most cavity-nesting birds lay one egg each morning and return to start incubating them once the clutch is completed (usually four or five days). This way the eggs all develop at the same rate and hatch synchronously.

Chickadees

Q: I recently put out a wren house and a pair of chickadees started going back and forth with bits of moss. I thought they were moving in. We went on a trip, and when we returned there was no sign of the chickadees. Did they abandon the site ? Should I clean the house out and hope for other tenants? D.G., KENTUCKY

A: Your chickadees may still be in residence but acting very sneaky, especially if they already have eggs in the nest box. (Note: Chickadees bury their eggs in the soft nest lining until incubation starts.) If they are gone, it's hard to tell why. If you check inside the box and find warm eggs, they are still using the box. If you can't get into the box, monitor it carefully for a few more days, especially in the early morning, to be sure the birds are not still active. If you see no activity for several days, remove the old nest and clean out the nest box.

Dryer lint

Q: I have always heard that dryer lint is good nesting material, but now people say it isn't. Why? P.V., PENNSYLVANIA

A: Lint is not good nesting material because it retains much more water than grass. Wet nesting material will not maintain the nest temperature as dry material will, and saturated nesting material can also cause a nest to lose its form. Wadded grass will regain its shape when it dries out, but dryer lint will not.

Wasp problems

Q: For the past two years large wasps have built small hanging nests in my nest boxes. What can

I do to evict them for good? T.R., NORTH CAROLINA

A: Remove the nest with a long stick and coat the ceiling of the box with petroleum jelly. You might also try hanging a few mothballs in a porous cloth bag in the nest box until the wasps leave. The vapors won't kill the wasps, but will discourage them. Don't use a plastic mesh bag, because mothball chemicals can escape through the openings.

Bird nests and the law

Q: We had robins, flycatchers, swallows, and house finches build nests around our house. Now that they're gone we'd like to paint the house, but we've heard that federal law prohibits disturbing birds' nests. What do we do? H.N., PENNSYLVANIA

A: Federal laws regarding nests were enacted to protect birds from egg collectors, plume sellers, and market hunters—not from people wanting to paint their houses.

Once birds finish with a nest, it is deemed inactive and abandoned. Even though some birds will use old nests in subsequent years, they are attracted more to the site than to the old nests. You may remove abandoned nests.

Unusual nest

Q: Recently a friend found a unique nest on his farm. It's made of twigs and grass and resembles a pouch. It's about three inches across at the opening and seven inches long. It even has a handle like string that attaches it to the tree. What bird might have constructed such a beautiful nest? J.H., TENNESSEE

A: The nest sounds like a Baltimore oriole nest. A good resource for you is *A Field Guide to Birds' Nests*, by Hal Harrison. It's part of the Peterson Field Guide Series from Houghton-Mifflin.

FYI

For more information about bluebirds, see ***Enjoying Bluebirds More,*** by Julie Zickefoose from BWD Press, and contact the North American Bluebird Society, Inc. at **www.nabluebirdsociety.org/** on the Internet.

Clean out box?

Q: My bluebirds just fledged from my nest box. Should I clean it our or will they use the old nest for another family? D.S., NEW YORK

A: Feel free to clean out the old nest. Any birds reusing the box will likely build a new nest anyway. In fall take out the old nest, but fashion a new one from dried grass. This gives winter birds roosting in the box a bit of cold-weather insulation.

Nest box competitors

Q: How can I keep other birds out of my bluebird boxes?A.C., WASHINGTON

A: Bluebirds, wrens, swallows, chickadees, nuthatches, and a few other birds naturally compete for nesting space. If you have several species competing for one nest box, hang more boxes in pairs. Let the swallows, for example, have one box and the bluebirds the other.

Dead swallows

Q: A tree swallow claimed our nest box, but something went wrong, and we found it dead in the box. What could we have done differently to prevent this? B.R., MICHIGAN

A: Tree swallows, with their early migration, often arrive on the breeding grounds before enough insect prey is available. Having short, weak legs, they are often unable to climb out of nest boxes, especially deep ones. Score the inside of the door below the hole to aid them in climbing out or mount the box so it slants forward, making it easier for swallows to climb to the exit hole.

Abandoned nest

Q: During March I put up six bluebird boxes. All but two were used. In May pairs began building in those, too. By June both of these pairs had built a nest and laid a clutch of eggs. I checked them both about three or four days prior to hatching. One had no eggs left and the other only had one egg. Could they have abandoned them? M.D., KENTUCKY

A: Missing bluebird eggs have usually been taken by wrens seeking to take over the box. Black rat snakes also take eggs. Be sure your nest boxes are fitted with snake-proof predator baffles and mounted well out in the open to discourage house wrens. For baffle plans, see *Enjoying Bluebirds More*. (See the outside back cover.)

MARIE READ

Tree swallows prefer to line their nests with white bird feathers.

Additional nestings

Q: How can I encourage bluebirds to nest a second or even third time? J.H., ONTARIO, CANADA

A: Birds at higher elevations and latitudes generally do not nest as many times each breeding season as their kin at lower elevations and latitudes. At your latitude, you can reasonably expect second nestings. Making additional nesting space available is a good start. Hanging a house toward the end of the nesting period might be a good way to avoid having wrens and swallows find it before the bluebirds are ready to use it.

Bird Behavior

Mate for life?

Q: Do all birds mate for life? C.Z., Nevada

A: No. Some species, such as some eagles, cranes, swans, geese, and ravens, have unusually strong pair bonds between mated birds that may last for life. Most North American bird species pair up primarily to reproduce and go their separate ways soon after nesting. In some species, such as the ruby-throated hummingbird, the pair bond is very brief, lasting only as long as courtship and copulation. The male has nothing to do with the incubation or raising of the young birds.

Migration

Q: Do all birds migrate? P.C., Oklahoma

A: No, but most do. Migration is defined as the seasonal movement north in the spring from the wintering grounds and southward in the fall from the breeding grounds. Among the resident, or nonmigratory, birds are many grouse, ptarmigan, and quail species; many owl species; pileated, red-bellied, downy, and hairy woodpeckers; white-breasted nuthatch; Carolina wren; northern cardinal; wrentit; ring-necked pheasant; Townsend's solitaire; common raven; gray jay; and northern mockingbird.

Courtship flight

Q: In July I observed an American goldfinch start from the ground in a field and fly circles, slowly rising to about 30 feet in the air. While the bird was doing this, it sang. Could this be a courtship display? T.P., Kentucky

CHARLES MELTON

A: Yes. Aerial displays and flight songs are basic components of many birds' courtship rituals. Because goldfiches delay nesting until weed seeds ripen, July is prime time for such courtship displays in goldfinches.

Courtship feeding

Q: While watching a couple of house finches at a tree near my feeders, I noticed the male come to my feeder and eat some seed, but the female didn't. After eating awhile, the male returned to the female. Then the male and female touched bills, and it looked like the male was regurgitating food into the mouth of the female. What was happening? M.R., Connecticut

A: If both birds were adults you were witnessing courtship behavior, in which a male feeds a female to demonstrate his intentions and show his prowess as a food gatherer.

If the "female" was actually a young house finch, you were witnessing an adult feeding its offspring. With house finches it can

Solicitous male northern cardinals reinforce pair bonds through courtship feeding.

be hard to determine what you witnessed, because young birds look very much like adult females.

Mobbing hawks

Q: Often when I see hawks, they are being hassled by American crows or other blackbirds. Is this a common phenomenon, and why it does occur? D.W., MICHIGAN

A: Mobbing behavior by crows is very common. The crows are reacting to the potential threat the hawk poses (as a predator) to them and their offspring. The mobbing often serves to harass the hawk into leaving the area. Occasionally a mobbed hawk will turn the tables and attack and kill a crow.

Flock noise

Q: I have often noticed that when little birds come through my yard in small flocks I hear lots of cheeping that isn't like their regular songs. Are these birds actually talking to each other? F.H., INDIANA

A: The cheeping you describe is a chorus of short, single, high-pitched notes uttered at intervals by each member of the flock. These calls make locating the bird extremely difficult for predators—and bird watchers—but allow the birds to keep track of flockmates without having to watch them. The birds can move together in the same direction while they keep their eyes open for danger and for food.

Dust bathing

Q: I noticed a bird flopping around in the dirt beneath my lilac hedge. I thought that someone had shot it or that it had escaped from a cat. When I went outside to rescue it, the bird flew off as if completely unharmed.

What in the world was it doing? N.H., MASSACHUSETTS

A: Birds clean dirt from their feathers by bathing in water, but they clean off parasites by bathing in dust. Flopping in fine soil coats their feathers with dust, which enters the breathing tubes of feather lice and feather mites. If these tubes become clogged, the lice and mites die. Their only defense is to drop off the dust-bathing bird.

Robins and spring

Q: There were more than 40 robins in our snow-covered backyard this January. I know that robins overwinter in the North, but to have seen so many seems to indicate migrating flocks. Could that be? L.B., MICHIGAN

A: American robins are surprisingly hardy as long as they have access to their winter food sources: berries and fruits. Robins are facultative migrants, meaning that they will migrate only as far south as they need to or are forced to by bad weather or food shortages. During ice storms, when berries and fruit are covered in a thick coating of ice, many robins flock together and move south. The idea that robins are the true first sign of spring is somewhat mythical. In much of northern North America, a few robins overwinter, but they stick to the woods and thickets where they can find fruit and berries. Most backyard bird watchers notice the robins' return when these birds appear on lawns with the onset of warm weather, seeking their warm-weather food: earthworms, grubs, caterpillars, and other insects.

Birds eating birds

Q: Wrens nested in a birdhouse that hangs in the tree in my front yard. About a week after the nestlings hatched, I noticed the wrens were very agitated and I looked out to see a blue jay trying to get into the house. Then I saw it pull away and it had what looked like a baby bird in its mouth. Do blue jays eat other birds? Is there anything I can do to protect the nestlings, or should I let nature take its course? K.L., OHIO

A: Yes, blue jays will eat other birds, especially nestlings. One way to prevent them from getting at baby birds is to use boxes with an extra ¾ inch thick block of wood over the entrance hole. This increases the distance a blue jay has to reach to get at the nest. Or you can use use very deep boxes, ones with at least 6 to 8 inches of interior wall beneath the entry hole.

Nest site fidelity

Q: We have several birdhouses in the yard of our Pennsylvania summer home. Are the bluebirds that stop in fall the young from that summer that were raised in these houses? J.F., ARIZONA

A: Some birds show little site fidelity to the areas where they were hatched or raised. Other birds (ospreys) exemplify the opposite extreme by returning to nearly the exact spot where they began life. Your bluebirds may be the same young that were hatched in your yard or they could be birds from elsewhere looking for new territories. Studies show that male bluebirds are site faithful, but females tend to disperse.

MASLOWSKI PHOTOGRAPHY

American robins can survive harsh winter weather if natural food sources, such as fruits and berries, are available.

Swift behavior

Q: Every night about 8 o'clock small birds fly in droves over our chimney. One at a time will go into the chimney until they all have had their turn. We have counted as many as 180 dropping into the chimney every night. What are these birds? J.K., MAINE

A: The birds are chimney swifts, named for their preferred nesting and roosting location inside chimneys. During migration they may form large nighttime roosts of several hundred, or even thousands. For more information Check your local library for a good bird book, such as Terres's *Audubon Encyclopedia of North American Birds*, where you'll find information on the species' natural history and behavior.

Preening behavior

Q: I saw a pair of American crows perched at the top of a snag, and one appeared to be grooming/ massaging/stroking the other. The groomer ran the tip of its bill along the top side of the neck of the second, through the feathers, starting at the nape and going up to the back of the head while the other bird hung its head. This was repeated about 5 times. Next the groomer ran the tip of its bill up the bottom side of the neck of the second, also through the feathers, from breast to chin. This was repeated about five times as well. What was happening? A.S., VIRGINIA

A: Ornithologists call this allo-preening and it occurs in a wide variety of birds including finches, parrots, raptors, and crows. It is a ritualized form of agonistic behavior that apparently bridges the gap between aggressive attacks and sexual behavior.

Bird Problems

Window strikes

Q: How can I keep birds from flying into my windows? D.A., VIRGINIA

A: Silhouettes of flying hawks or falcons do work, but they perform best when applied on the outside of the glass. Hanging ornaments such as wind chimes, wind socks, and potted plants in front of windows also helps. Misting the outside of the window with a very weak detergent or soda solution will eliminate the reflection but will also impair visibility for you. Awnings, eave extensions, and window screens will eliminate all reflection and stop the collision problem. Plastic cling wrap applied to the inside or outside of the window can also be effective. Learn how to build your own FeatherGuard (see sidebar). They are one of the best ways to prevent window strikes.

JAMIE HARRON

A male indigo bunting attacks its reflection in an old truck mirror.

Bird reflections

Q: We have a female cardinal that has declared war on our house. She starts whacking herself into our windows at 6 a.m. and will not quit until the sun goes down. How long will this behavior last? K.T., OHIO

A: The behavior will last through the breeding season. In some individuals it may go on year-round, for years. It's a territorial reaction to seeing an intruder on her "turf." Covering the windows with screens will help, but the bird may just move to another window. You might try screening or plastic wrap on the outside surfaces of the window. Remove any perches from which the bird can see itself in the windows. And continue to harass the bird to try to shock it out of its pattern of territoriality. (Spraying the bird with the garden hose may work, and rubber snakes hung by the windows sometimes do the trick.) If all else fails, call your local

Reduce Window Kills

FeatherGuard is easy to make, costs little, and is attractive, but not to birds. I make them in less than 10 minutes per window, and you can, too. Try it on windows that get hit the most. The only materials required are monofilament fishing line and feathers. You can buy a bag of feathers at a local crafts store—medium-sized feathers (about six to eight inches long) work best.

STILES THOMAS

Domestic bird feathers tied to vertically hung strings seem to warn other birds away.

Step one: Measure the window from top to bottom. Add two feet to the measurement to allow for fastening to the house and to allow FeatherGuard to blow in the wind.

Step two: Drill a 1⁄16-inch hole (1.5 mm) in the feather shaft at about the center of gravity.

Step three: Thread the feather and slide it to the middle of the line. Then tie a simple knot to keep it in place. Next, slide on another two feathers about seven inches on each side of the first and tie in place. Attach the remaining feathers until you've got a feather every seven inches or so. Don't forget to leave a foot or so at each end to fasten the rig to the top and bottom of your window. All measurements are approximate.

Step four: Tap a long flathead nail into the window frame above and below the window so the nail protrudes two or three inches from the frame. This will keep the feathers away from the glass. The nail should be perpendicular to the frame so the line doesn't slide. Then secure the line at the nail head. There should only be enough slack to permit the FeatherGuard to sway from one side of the glass to the other. That's all there is to it.—*Stiles Thomas*

wildlife officials and ask them to come out and remove the bird for you. It's drastic, but it will end the problem for good.

Woodpeckers on siding

Q: I have a woodpecker that is pecking holes in my house siding. Is there anything I can do to get him to stop? D.M., PENNSYLVANIA

A: A woodpecker drilling on your wooden house is only doing what comes naturally to it—drilling into wood in search of shelter or food. Most house-wrecking woodpeckers do their damage in the fall, which is when they begin making their winter roost holes. Try mounting a nest box with an appropriately-sized hole over the drilled area. Fill the house with woodchips, and you may divert the bird's attention and gain a tenant. In spring woodpeckers also use wood and sometimes metal parts of houses as drumming sites to announce their territory and attract a mate. There are several things you can try.

- Place some sheet metal or heavy aluminum foil over the area the bird is using.
- Hang some aluminum pie plates around the affected area. Make sure they move in the wind to scare the bird.
- Place a rubber snake near the drilling area.
- Repeatedly scare the bird when it lands on your house.
- If nothing else works, call your local wildlife official, who may come to your house to remove the offending bird.

Dead crows

Q: We found two dead crows in the street in front of our house. What killed them? E.G., GEORGIA

A: If you found the birds in the road they were most likely killed by cars while eating roadkill—perhaps they were young, inexperienced birds. However, there is reason to be careful around dead crows. In recent years American crows have been dying from West Nile virus. If you find any more dead crows, call your local wildlife officials and have the crows tested for this disease. West Nile can be transmitted to humans, but only via mosquito bite. Contact your local health department for information about any occurrence of West Nile in your area.

Snakes and birds

Q: A snake ate my bluebirds right out of the box. How can I prevent this? R.F., MONTANA

A: Pole-mounted baffles are the only way to keep snakes and most other predators from getting to a box full of bluebirds. Unbaffled boxes mounted on fenceposts or trees offer no protection against natural predators. For a baffle design you can build, see *Enjoying Bluebirds More* by BWD Press (see this booklet's outside back cover), or ask your local specialty bird store about pole-mounted baffles.

Headless birds

Q: I keep finding decapitated birds in my yard. What's doing it? B.W., KANSAS

A: In urban and suburban settings grackles are the most likely culprits, although jays, magpies, and crows will decapitate small birds, too. Screech-owls and pygmy-owls also decapitate their prey, but, intending to eat them later, they usually cache their victims out of sight.

Nocturnal bird song

Q: Every spring I have a bird that sings not only throughout the day, but all night long. I love the sound of birds, but this drives me nuts! This bird has many different songs. What is it and what can I do about it? B.H., CALIFORNIA

A: Your bird is most likely a northern mockingbird. Don't worry, male mockingbirds perform

MASLOWSKI PHOTOGRAPHY

Northern mockingbirds will defend a food source in winter.

this nocturnal singing only in spring, during a full moon. I suggest running an electric fan (to create a buffer of sound) and using your earplugs on nights when the mockingbird is singing. Having a mocker around is a good thing—you might even consider yourself lucky!

Killing birds

Q: We have a problem with a neighborhood boy who shoots birds with his BB gun. I went out one day last winter to find him with a pile of 15 to 20 dead birds. Are there any laws against this? O.B., TEXAS

A: International treaties protect most birds. Some birds are exempted from the treaties, however, most of these are regulated as game species that may be shot only in designated seasons by people who purchase the required licenses. But rock doves, European starlings, and house sparrows are exempted as nonnative species, and therefore no season or license is required to kill them. *All* migratory songbirds are protected, and it is illegal to shoot them in any season.

Killing a bird protected by treaty is a federal offense. Also, most municipalities have ordinances against discharging firearms within city limits and against harming birds. The boy could be violating several laws at various government levels. Call your state wildlife agency to ask that an officer speak to the boy and his parents.

Stuck starlings

Q: Twice in the past month I have traced a noise to a starling stuck in a downspout leading from my roof gutter. What's going on with the starlings, and how can I keep them out of there? P.A., CALIFORNIA

A: Because they nest and roost in cavities and will use almost any enclosed space, starlings are keenly motivated to investigate dark blotches that could be holes.

Furthermore, starlings use roof gutters as a source of water for drinking and bathing, which puts them in a position to see the hole where the gutter drains into the downspout.

Predictably, a young starling—which yours probably is—will peek into a downspout and commit itself to explore. The same thing happens with stovepipes, chimneys, and vents. A sheet of galvanized wire mesh attached over the gutter and above the downspout juncture will exclude the starlings.

Sick/Injured/ Orphaned Birds

Banded birds

Q: I found a bird with a band on its leg. What should I do? B.T., WASHINGTON

A: Report all birds with bands or tags to the Bird Banding Laboratory at the Patuxent Wildlife Center at 800-327-2263 or **www.pwrc.usgs.gov/** on the Internet. The lab will take the report and pass it on to the bird's bander. Eventually (it can take a while), you will get a note telling you where and when the bird was originally banded.

Injured birds

Q: I found an injured bird. What should I do with it? T.H., OHIO

A: Special permits from the federal, state, or provincial government are required to handle injured or dead nongame bird species. Whereas your first instinct may be to call your local veterinarian, many are unwilling to care for wildlife cases. Often the best thing to do is to let nature take its course. As part of nature's natural cycle of life and death, an injured or dead bird may be a meal for another animal. If you feel you must do something to help an injured bird, call your local wildlife office, department of the environment, fish and game or extension office, who may know of a licensed rehabilitator in your area.

Sick house finches

Q: I have seen two house finches with red, swollen eyes at my feeder. They don't seem to be able to see very well and they don't fly away when I get near them. What is wrong with them? D.G., VIRGINIA

A: It sounds like the birds may be suffering from House Finch Disease (mycoplasmal conjunctivitis). House finches are not the only birds to get the disease, but it spreads more rapidly among them because they tend to flock at feeders more than some other birds.

Take down your feeders and clean them with a ten percent bleach solution (one part bleach and nine parts water). Let them dry completely and then re-hang them. Rake underneath the feeder to remove old seed and bird droppings.

Cornell University is conducting a House Finch Disease survey to track the spread of the disease in the United States. For more information or to participate in the survey, go to **http://birds.cornell.edu/hofi/** on the Internet or call 800-843-2473.

LANCE BEENY

RICHARD DAY/DAYBREAK IMAGERY

Top: A sick house finch. Sick birds often appear puffed up and listless.
Bottom: A fledgling killdeer. Killdeer young are able to walk and forage almost immediately.

Fallen nestlings

Q: If I find a young bird that has fallen from a nest, what should I do? S.P., Georgia

A: Try to place the nestling back in its nest if at all possible. This will be the young bird's best chance at a for survival. If you can't find the nest or a place to put the nestling out of harm's way, you will need to get the bird to a licensed rehabilitator as soon as possible. Baby birds are unable to thermoregulate (regulate their body temperature), so they must be kept in a protected area with a heat source. A soft nest made of tissues inside a small cardboard box, placed on a heating pad set on LOW, is a good temporary home. A moist sponge placed in the box will add a touch of desired humidity.

Your state or provincial fish and wildlife officers are responsible for licensing and regulating the activities of rehabilitators and have listings for all rehabbers in your state.

If a fledgling is found hopping around on the ground, it should be left alone if it's in a safe area. It can be placed up on a tree branch or in a shrub if in a dangerous situation but must remain in the same area so its parents can find it. Birds have an underdeveloped sense of smell, so handling the baby bird won't cause the parents to abandon it. Young birds often leave the nest before they are capable of flight. They spend a few pre-flight days hopping on the ground and flapping their wings. Its parents are keeping an eye on it and feeding it when necessary. During this time the fledgling is learning valuable survival lessons from its parents.

Emergency food for nestlings

If you find an orphaned nestling songbird and there's no licensed rehabilitator immediately available to receive the youngster, here is a recipe for basic baby bird care.

Grind up dry dog food into a powder. Add warm water to make a yogurtlike slurry. Offer it to the bird through a baby medicine syringe, gently prying the bill open. Keep the bird warm in a tissue nest inside a box. If necessary, use a warm water bottle or heating pad on low placed nearby. As soon as possible get the bird to a wildlife rehabilitator.

BIRDS NEED WATER YEAR-ROUND

Birdbaths

Attracting birds

Q: How can I get the birds to notice my wonderful new birdbath? P.H., MONTANA

A: Add motion to the water. Moving water, caused by a mister or dripping hose system is irresistible to birds. You can even find birdbaths with recirculating and heating features built in. For a cheap dripper, suspend a milk jug full of water over your birdbath. Poke small holes in the bottom and top until the jug produces a regular drip.

Bleach

Q: Would it be harmful to the birds to add a little household bleach to the water in my birdbath? S.H., ALASKA

A: Chlorine kills living creatures. That's why we put it in water—to kill the bacteria, fungi, algae, and protozoans that can sicken or even kill us. Our bodies can cope with the small amount of chlorine we add to water far more easily than they can with the toxins produced by these microbes.

The issue of chlorine and birds is one of how much is enough. People often believe that if a little is good, more is better, which is seldom the case. One tablespoon of liquid chlorine bleach in about three gallons of tepid water will meet most health codes for human sanitization. One cup of liquid chlorine bleach in nine cups of water (a 1:9 ratio) is an accepted disinfecting solution for feeders and birdbaths. Be sure to rinse well. To control algae in birdbaths, this rule of thumb is helpful: If you can smell the chlorine in the water, you've added enough bleach.

Location

Q: How far from trees and plants should a birdbath be placed? H.N., MINNESOTA

A: Near enough to offer shelter for the birds but far enough away that the droppings of perched birds don't fall into the water.

Painting birdbaths

Q: I have three birdbaths in my yard—two shallow ones and one with a deeper bowl. All three of them are concrete, and I'm thinking of painting them. Will painting them make it easier to keep them clean, or should I just leave them alone? B.Y., WASHINGTON

A: I don't think painting your concrete birdbaths will make them easier to clean. You may want to clean and scrub them regularly using a light bleach-water mixture—a cup of bleach to two gallons of water. Make sure you scrub the scum off the bath surface and then rinse and refill with clean water.

NED HARRIS

Moving water, caused by a dripper system, attracted this female Gambel's quail to a backyard birdbath.

Birdbaths in winter

Q: I'm getting mixed information about birdbaths in winter. It gets pretty cold around here, so some people say don't put water out. Others say water is important. So which is it? B.G., COLORADO

A: Birds need water. Clean feathers are warm feathers. If birds cannot get water from your yard, they will find it elsewhere. Typical urban sources of winter include snowmelt puddles in the street and roof gutters. Whether it's in a garden water feature or a simple birdbath, keep water unfrozen any of these ways:

• A water pump that circulates the water

• An air pump that vigorously aerates the water

• A submersible water heater

• If you choose a submersible heater, use only a model with a thermostat that will turn the heater off when the water heats up sufficiently. They cost more but are much cheaper and far safer to operate. Make sure you plug your heater into a grounded outdoor plug with a ground fault interrupter to avoid electric shock.

• Avoid metal birdbath components to prevent wet feathers and toes from freezing to them.

Dust bath

Q: I want to make a dust bath for birds in my backyard. What dust is good and safe for birds and exactly how do I make it? L.M., SOUTH CAROLINA

A: Make the dust out of the earth you have on site. After several days of dry weather, till a patch until it is crumbled into fine particles. Pick a sandy or already open, dusty spot for a dustbath. Alternatively, you can dig a shallow hole (2 inches deep) about 2 feet by 2 feet and fill it with fine-grained sand.

HEALTHY, HAPPY HUMMERS

Hummingbirds

Feeding solution

Q: What is the best sugar-to-water ratio to use for feeding hummingbirds? N.Z., Florida

A: Four parts water to one part sugar (a 4:1 ratio) has been shown to be the closest to the sucrose content of natural flower nectar. Concentrations stronger than this (3:1 ratio, and stronger) are readily consumed by hummers, but no scientific evidence exists regarding the potential helpful or harmful effects the birds.

Q: When making hummingbird solution, do I boil the water before or after I add the sugar? M.L., New Mexico

A: If you are using chlorinated municipal water, boiling helps to reduce the amount of chlorine present in the water. Cool your solution before giving the birds access to it. If you boil the water, do it first, before adding the sugar.

Other sweeteners

Q: Can I use molasses or honey instead of sugar to make my hummer nectar? C.L., Vermont

A: No. White table sugar is the only commercial sweetener that, when mixed with the right amount of water, closely resembles natural flower nectar. Resist the urge to use other sweeteners, which spoil quickly and may not be good for the birds.

Q: Regarding a hummingbird feeding solution, is there any nutritional benefit from using bottled spring water or brown sugar instead of tap water and granulated white sugar? D.S., California

A: No known plant makes its nectar with brown sugar, and neither should you.

Regarding bottled water, the answer is more equivocal. "Spring" water is not necessarily pure water; neither chlorine nor fluoride, as additives to municipal water supplies, is as harmful as many people believe. Anyone whose tap water is tainted by sulfur or calcium compounds would probably see more hummingbird activity by either filtering the water with a commercial filtration device or using bottled water.

Red dye

Q: Is the red dye that is found in premixed hummer solution bad for the birds? L.M., Maine

A: Although there is no conclusive evidence that red food dye is harmful to hummingbirds, this chemical additive is not necessary in their feeding solution. Many commercial brands of solution contain the coloring, which is meant to be attractive both to hummingbirds and to shopping bird watchers (brightly colored flowers are

A male broad-tailed hummingbird at a penstemon flower.

nature's way of attracting a foraging hummingbird). Red feeder parts (which most hummer feeders have) or a bright red ribbon hung near the feeder can be just as attractive as red-dyed solution.

Aggressive hummers

Q: How do I foil a "bully" hummer? M.H., New York

A: Many hummingbird species defend feeding territories, and assemblages at feeders usually develop hierarchies. The behavior exemplifies natural selection at work, and you should do nothing except enjoy it. If you're worried about hungry hummers, put up several more feeders near the original one. The bully will be overwhelmed by sheer numbers of other birds and will be less territorial.

Ants and bees

Q: How do I keep ants and bees out of the hummingbird feeder? C.D., Arizona

A: Select a hummingbird feeder with bee guards, which prevent bees and yellow jackets from drinking, and replace feeders that drip. You can discourage ants from getting to your hummer food by painting laundry detergent on the surface the ants use to reach the feeder (don't paint the feeder). The solution interferes with the ants' chemical navigation. Refresh the application several times the first day. After a few days, you won't need it anymore.

Courtship display

Q: Why does a male hummer fly in a U-shaped pattern? W.R., Arkansas

A: Male hummingbirds perform a variety of courtship displays. This is the pendulum display flight of a male hummer to a perched female. He zips back and forth and flashes his colorful throat (gorget) at her, hoping to impress her into mating with him. It is common to see this behavior in early summer.

Migration myths

Q: Do hummingbirds migrate on the backs of Canada geese? V.P., New Hampshire

A: No. This is either a Native American myth or just an old wives' tale. Hummingbirds are excellent, strong-flying migrants. A healthy ruby-throated hummingbird can easily handle the 500-mile flight across the Gulf of Mexico.

Q: Is it true that hummingbirds at my feeder will not migrate if I leave my feeder up in the fall? M.S., IDAHO

A: No. This is another in a long line of bird myths. Birds are genetically programmed to migrate when their internal "clocks" tell them to do so. They will depart when the time is right whether your feeders are up or not. However, leaving your feeders up in the fall and getting them up early in the spring may help late or early migrants that are passing through your area.

Spoiled feeding solution

Q: What causes the cloudiness in my hummingbird sugar-water solution? How can I prevent this from happening? B.L., VIRGINIA

A: The cloudiness in your solution is caused by bacterial development, which is hastened by the warm sunlight striking the slowly fermenting sugar water. Impurities in your water and in the sugar are the starting points for this bacterial or fungal development. One way to slow this process is to add the sugar to boiling water, rather than to lukewarm tap water. Stir in the sugar and wait until the solution comes to another boil before turning off the heat and letting the solution cool down to room temperature. Store excess solution in your refrigerator in a clean plastic container.

HERBERT CLARKE

Male Calliope hummingbirds vie for space at a crowded hummer feeder.

Here are some other tips that might might help.

• Place your feeder or feeders in a shady location.

• Run your feeders though your dishwasher once a week. Don't use a high heat setting if your feeders are made of thin plastic.

• Get an easy to clean feeder. Sometimes the bacteria can hide in crevices, scratches, and other hard-to-reach places in a standard feeder.

• Consider filling your feeders with just enough solution for a day or two, so the hummers drink it up before it can spoil.

• Soak your feeders in hot, soapy water each time you refill them. Use a feeder-cleaning brush or pipe cleaners to get all the gunk out of the feeder ports.

Finches at feeders

Q: My hummer feeders have been taken over by house finches.